IMAGES
of Wales

GRANGETOWN
THE SECOND SELECTION

Bicycles and the electric tramcar were the most common forms of transport in this view of an almost traffic-free Clare Road, *c.* 1920.

IMAGES
of Wales

GRANGETOWN
THE SECOND SELECTION

Compiled by
Ian Clarke

TEMPUS

First published 1999
Copyright © Ian Clarke, 1999

Tempus Publishing Limited
The Mill, Brimscombe Port,
Stroud, Gloucestershire, GL5 2QG

ISBN 0 7524 1553 0

Typesetting and origination by
Tempus Publishing Limited
Printed in Great Britain by
Midway Clark Printing, Wiltshire

I would like to dedicate this book to my children:
Leigh, Sophie, Lucy, Thomas, and Ross as a lasting reminder of their rich heritage.

Contents

This year, 1999, marked the centenary of Ebenezer Gospel Hall on Corporation Road which opened on 5 October 1899 to replace earlier premises which had fallen into disrepair in Eleanor Place and Evelyn Street at Cardiff Docks. The hall was built at a cost of £1,250 and consisted of a main hall to seat 500 people, classrooms and a large basement hall. During the Second World War the basement was used as an ARP shelter and on the night of 2 January 1941 over 140 local children were enjoying a Sunday school tea when there was a heavy bombing raid on the area. All were safe, but for the next few weeks over 100 people were accommodated at the hall, having been evacuated from nearby homes after bomb damage.

Introduction

Grange Farm has existed on the West Moors since around 1200 when the monks of Margam Abbey were granted lands for farming. The farm remained an isolated smallholding for many centuries until the middle of the nineteenth century when housing development commenced and the district of Cardiff known as Grangetown was born. Building began in two separate areas: the Thomas Street and Penarth Road area in Upper Grangetown and Earl and Kent Street in Lower Grangetown, and was to provide housing for workers and tradesmen working in the newly opened Bute Docks.

Lord Windsor, the landowner for lower Grangetown who lived in Worcestershire, decided that many of the streets should bear names associated with his family home. These were Holmesdale, Amherst, Knole, Hewell, Oakley and Bromsgrove.

In the years 1885 to 1888 the well-known local businessman Solomon Andrews constructed three rows of terraced houses between Clive Street and Kent Street and named them: Andrews Terrace, Fair View and Sea View but they were later incorporated into Ferry Road. Solomon Andrews also ran horse buses along Ferry Road to its furthest point at the mouth of the River Ely where a chain link ferry service operated to Penarth Dock. The ferry service had started in 1865 but could not be used at low tide or in rough weather.

The Taff Vale Railway Company, who exported coal from Penarth Dock, decided to build a public subway under the River Ely. The subway was of tubular design and lined with six cylindrical caste iron sections which were 10ft in external diameter. The walls were 18ins wide and were bolted together. Work commenced in April 1897 at the Ferry Road end and by 1 July 1897 a trench had been completed to take the first sections of lining, which were installed by steam crane. The final sections at the Penarth end were also laid in a trench. All these sections were covered and protected by brickwork which, at the Ferry Road end, still exist. The two trenches were connected by means of tunnelling through the river banks and below the river bed, the lowest section being 11ft below the river.

The subway, costing £36,203, was opened on Monday 14 May 1900 by Mrs Beasley, wife of the general manager of the Taff Vale Railway Company. It was well used by dock workers and local residents for many years, but with the decline of Penarth Dock it gradually fell into disuse and was closed on 30 September 1963. Penarth Motorboat and Sailing Club occupy the Ferry Road site and the Penarth Dock site has been redeveloped for housing.

After the success of an earlier Grangetown book in this series compiled by Barbara Jones an interest was rekindled in this forgotten district of the capital city of Wales. Many interesting photographs came to light and this book sets out to share more of this forgotten heritage.

Photographs of yesteryear give us an insight into a way of life long gone. They show happy, difficult and sad times which the community survived with spirit. Many of us are proud to be part of that spirit. Some photographs date from within living memory and others are before our time but they all provide an interesting window on the past. I was honoured to be asked to compile this second selection which proved to be a labour of love for an area so close to my heart.

Ian Clarke
March 1999

The Clarence Road Bridge over the River Taff between the new district of Grangetown and the docks was considered to be an engineering wonder when it opened in September 1890. The first electric tramcar service to use the bridge began on 2 May 1902 on the service from City Road via Wood Street and Clare Road to the docks.

One
Grangetown's Yesterdays

Workers pose in front of a 'hedge' of leather hides at the tannery on Sloper Road near the junction of Penarth Road in the early years of this century.

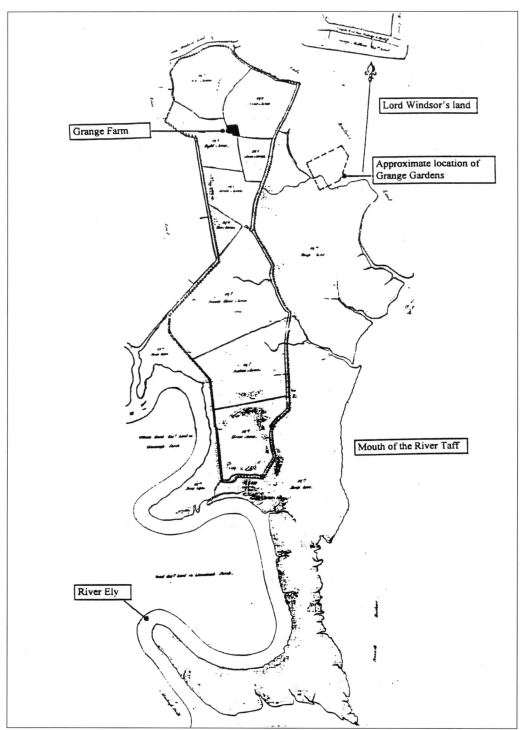

Grange Farm

Lord Windsor's land

Approximate location of
Grange Gardens

Mouth of the River Taff

River Ely

This 1766 map shows the extent of the lands of Grange Farm. This area between the River Taff and the River Ely formed the basis for the area now known as Grangetown.

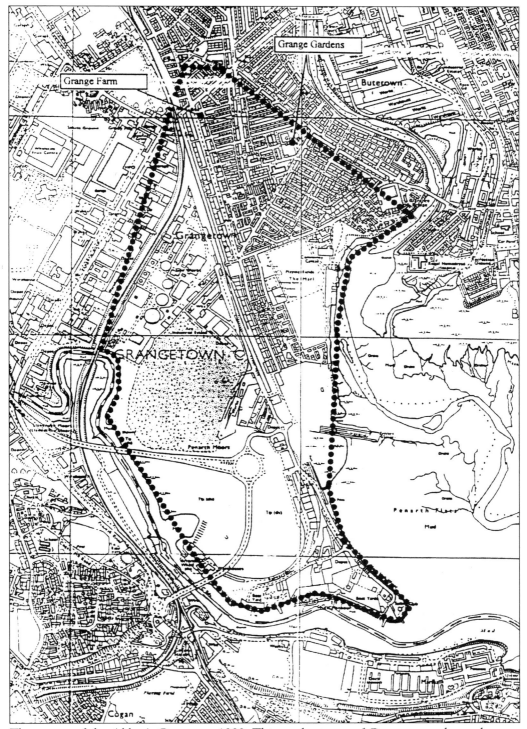

The extent of the Abbot's Grange, *c.* 1300. This modern map of Grangetown shows the area that the original farm occupied imposed on the street plan.

Grange Farm viewed from land to the rear of Grangetown library, *c.* 1920. By now the farm is surrounded by buildings.

Paget Street pictured just after the First World War.

A 1912 view of Corporation Road seen from the Penarth Road junction with the imposing frontage of the Forward Movement Presbyterian Hall seen to the right.

Children stand in a quiet Corporation Road in 1914.

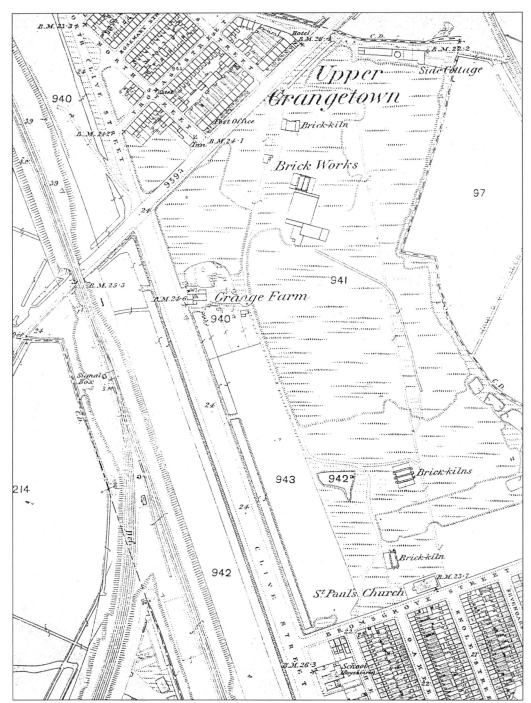

An Ordnance Survey map from 1880. This map shows how the development of Grangetown began in two separate areas, north of Penarth Road and south of Bromsgrove Street. This left the land surrounding Grange Farm virtually untouched.

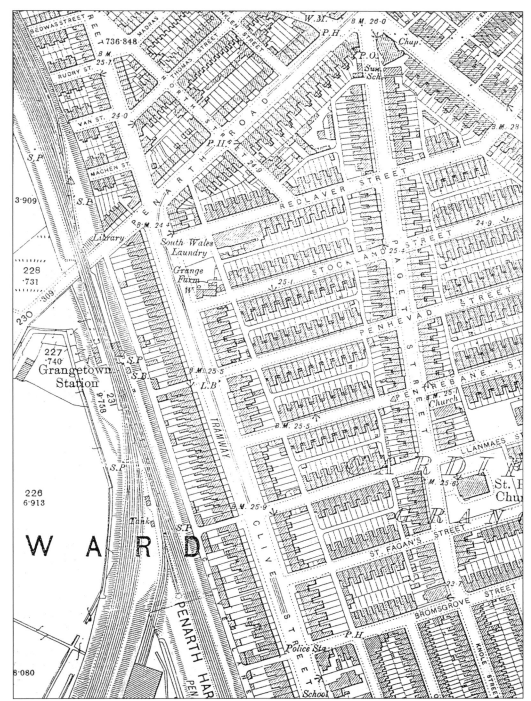

An Ordnance Survey map from 1901. In the space of just twenty years all the remaining land has been developed for housing and business premises. The farm building can still be seen on the corner of Clive Street and Stockland Street.

Grangetown Branch Library was originally situated at No. 1 Clive Street, a dwelling house bought by local brewery owner, Councillor Samuel A. Brain JP who donated it for use as a public library. In September 1901 Councillor Brain opened the new Grangetown Library which was next to Grange Farm. The land had been purchased at a cost of £520 and the building, designed by architect Colonel Bruce Vaughan, was constructed by building contractors D. Thomas & Sons at a cost of £3,521. Councillor Brain, who had already provided 3,000 volumes to form the foundation of the collection of books, was presented with a gold key as a memento of the event.

The Inn on the River public house was originally built by local builder, William Turner, as his home calling it Min Y Avon. It was later used as offices for the National Coal Board before being converted into a public house.

This is an architect's impression of the Clarence Bridge. The engineer was Mr W. Harpur MInst, CE. It was originally planned as the Grangetown Bridge but the change to the name was made to honour Queen Victoria's grandson the Duke of Clarence and Avondale who had agreed to preside over the opening ceremony of the bridge which took place on 17 September 1890.

Local youngsters pose on the bank of the River Taff, 18 September 1889. Behind them the construction of Clarence Bridge is well underway by Cardiff born contractor Charles Robert Hemingway.

The first of three sections of the bridge is in place as seen here on 18 September 1889.

Workmen stop to pose for the photographer on 11 February 1890. The scale of the bridge is apparent from this picture.

The bridge begins to take shape in this view from 20 March 1890. When completed it was 464ft 8ins in length and 40ft wide.

This employee, seen standing near the huge mechanism which swung the bridge open, shows the size of the workings of the bridge and gives an indication of the amount of work that was needed to complete this project.

The completed bridge had its road surface laid by steamroller to the interest of the watching crowd.

A tramcar, bound for the docks, can be seen approaching the finished Clarence Road Bridge in 1914.

The scene had changed little sixteen years later in 1930. Here, a No. 6 tramcar can be seen crossing Clarence Road Bridge from Grangetown.

After the demise of the tramcar, trolleybuses continued to use the bridge until 20 March 1966 when the last trolleybus, seen in this view, closed the service.

Progress, and volume of traffic, sadly necessitated the building of a new bridge which was constructed in 1976. It ran directly alongside the old bridge which can be seen being dismantled in this view. The Prime Minister the Rt Hon. James Callaghan, who was MP for Cardiff South, opened the new bridge on the 9 April 1976.

A chain ferry operated across the River Ely from Ferry Road to Penarth Dock up until the opening of the Taff Vale Railway subway in 1895. Solomon Andrews operated horse buses to the subway for workers to the Penath Docks and visitors to Penarth seafront.

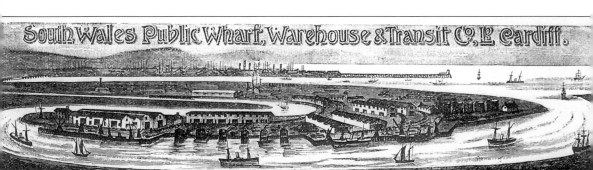

VICTORIA WHARVES.

At a time when Cardiff was the world's largest coal exporting port, the River Ely tidal harbour was used by the Taff Vale Railway to export coal from the South Wales valleys. This advertisement for South Wales Public Wharf, Warehouse & Transit Co. Ltd, showing Victoria Wharf, gives a good overview of the harbour and the buildings surrounded it.

The toll collector is seen standing at the gates of the Penarth Road tollgate some fifty years ago. Toll roads where privately owned roads, and passage along them was allowed by the payment of a toll.

A hearse pauses at the Penarth Road tollgate in the early 1950s.

In 1914 the Ninian Palace Cinema, which seated 600, opened as a silent film cinema with an orchestra of four musicians who played at the front of the auditorium hidden by a screen of velvet curtains. Popularly known as the 'Nin', several generations were entertained by all the great films that where shown there until 1972, when it became a bingo hall. The building is little changed today and is currently a retail furniture store.

Two
Trades and Businesses

W. SHEEHAN,

WHOLESALE & RETAIL

Hay, Straw, Corn & Seed Merchant,

PARAGON STORES,

146 Penarth Road, Cardiff.

Telephone No. 722.

HIGHEST Standard Quality

— AT —

LOWEST Possible Prices. :

FOODS, MEDICINES and REQUISITES

For HORSES, CATTLE, POULTRY, PIGEONS, DOGS, CAGE BIRDS, and ALL OTHER

——— LIVE STOCK.———

A Trial Order will Please me and Satisfy you.

W. Sheehan was an established hay, straw, corn and seed merchant at 146 Penarth Road in 1913. The advertisement shows that he also sold 'Food, Medicines & Requisites' for all types of live stock. An interesting footnote can be seen at the bottom of the advertisement.

BELLAMY'S
Chest Protector

Is a blend of the Finest Tinctures and Essences of Plants skilfully combined with PURE WELSH HONEY. It is guaranteed to cure the worst Cough in a very short time, and the first dose gives almost INSTANT RELIEF.

IT IS UNDOUBTEDLY THE BEST REMEDY KNOWN FOR CURING

COUGHS, COLDS, BRONCHITIS, ASTHMA
And all disorders of the THROAT and CHEST.

1/- per bottle; Three bottles for **2/6**

PREPARED ONLY BY—

A. J. BELLAMY, M.P.S.,

Nat Tel. 566. Chemist, PAGET STREET, CARDIFF.

An advertisement from 1913 for Bellamy's Chest Protector, a cough medicine sold at A.J. Bellamy's chemist shop on Paget Street.

Fred Saddler's shaving saloon occupied a building on Holmesdale Street, around 1900.

A tradecard for J. Witcomb, oil and colour merchant who traded from Penarth Road.

A tradecard for H. Hobbs, dyer and cleaner, who traded from Penarth Road and also had a shop on Albany Road in Roath.

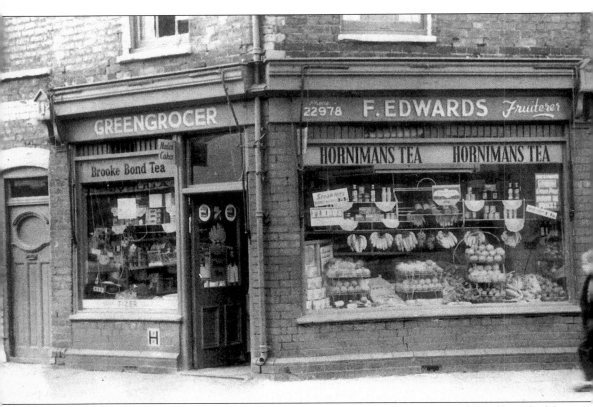

Often referred to as 'Poppy Whiting's shop', this view of F. Edwards shows the well stocked fruit and vegetable shop at The Square, Holmesdale Street, around 1960.

W. J. HALL,

BAKER,

PASTRYCOOK and CONFECTIONER,

Grangetown Steam Machine Bakery,

CORPORATION ROAD AND PENARTH ROAD,

Cardiff.

A tradecard for W.J. Hall's bakery on Corporation Road and Penarth Road.

Alec Foulkes' shoe shop at 66 Holmesdale Street in 1913/14.

Fish, poultry, fruit and vegetables are all displayed at A. Plain's shop at 21 Corporation Road. This shows the way that produce was displayed outside the shop, a far cry from the health and safety conscious shops of today.

W. HIGGINS,

DENTAL SURGERY

AT

27, CORPORATION ROAD.

Painless Extractions, 1/6 ; Gas, 2/6.

SETS from £1 1s. 0d.   SINGLE TOOTH from 2/6.

FITTINGS from 2/6.

CALL AND SEE TESTIMONIALS.

1913

A 1913 advertisement for W. Higgins dental surgery, at 27 Corporation Road.

Joseph Bann (second left) can be seen here posing with his children William, Harry and Alice outside his butcher's shop on Holmesdale Street around 1910.

A 1910 tradecard for F.E. Lewis grocer and provision merchant. As well as the shop in Corporation Road in Grangetown they also occupied premises in Cathays.

A tradecard for J.H. Geldard from 1910. As a baker and confectioner, they made and sold all sorts of cakes and sweets, from the shop and to order.

A couple of advertisements for Games Evans Ltd, City Drug Stores on Clare Road from 1913. The first advertises 'Balsam of Horehound' as a cough and cure-all. The second assures customers of the company's ability to dispense prescriptions.

This is a photograph of Games Evans' chemist shop situated on the corner of Clare Road and Cornwall Street around 1915.

A. J. KENDRICK

GENTLEMENS HAIRDRESSER
102 CLARE ROAD, CARDIFF
TEL. 1248

A.J. Kendrick's smart gentlemen's hairdressing shop, *c.* 1950. The telephone number for this Clare Road shop – 1248 – is reminiscent of simpler times.

A. J. KENDRICK

102 CLARE ROAD,
GRANGE, CARDIFF

First Class Gent's Hairdresser

Modern Four-Chair Saloon

All towels and implements regularly sterilised

High Class Toilet Requisites

CIGARETTES AND TOBACCO

This advertisement for Kendrick's, from 1950, shows the full range of services a hairdresser offered.

In 1933 Pidgeon's had a successful car hire service which included supplying cars for royal visits. They are now recognized as an established funeral business in Cardiff.

This and the following tradecard, from the 1940s, show the kind of vehicles that were available to hire from Pidgeon's Hire Service. The caption reads, 'This 50 H.P. Daimler may be hired at moderate rates from PIDGEON'S HIRE SERVICE. CLARE ROAD, CARDIFF'.

The caption on this tradecard reads: 'Pidgeon's Daimlers were chosen by this happy pair for their bridal carriages. May we place them at your disposal? PIDGEON'S HIRE SERVICE. 61 CLARE ROAD, CARDIFF.'

Girls from the New Era Laundry in Pendyris Street enjoying the sunshine during a work break, *c.* 1930.

Len Stevens, from lower Grangetown, master of the tugboat *Margaret Ham* in 1962.

The *Margaret Ham* entering Cardiff Docks, 1962.

Len Stevens (second left) pictured with crews employed by J. Davies (who owned a local tugboat company called Towage) in the 1950s.

Len Stevens as a boy is pictured second right aboard the tugboat *May* with tugmaster Bill Stevens (far right). This tug conveyed Gugliemo Marconi on his visits to the Flat Holm in 1897 where, on the 11 May, the first wireless message was transmitted across water to Lavernock.

Master Mariner Edwin Charles Phillips of Kent Street operated three tugboats in 1911 and continued successfully until the company ceased trading in the early 1930s.

The tugs *Sylph* and *Norman* were operated from Cardiff Docks by E.C. Phillips of Kent Street.

The Windsor Slipway & Dry Docks Company in Ferry Road was founded in 1882 and was situated at the entrance of the River Taff. It enabled ships to be repaired and avoid paying dock dues, as the dry docks were not within the confines of Bute Docks.

Ships under repair at the Windsor Slipway & Dry Dock Company. Today this site is occupied by the Windsor Quay housing development.

Staff employed by Joseph Lucas Ltd, Penarth Road, pictured in the 1950s. The building which housed this motor component company was demolished in 1999 for future redevelopment.

E. Gillard carriage business was based in Dorset Street before the First World War.

The Avana Associated Bakeries have long been established in Pendyris Street and this view, taken in the 1950s, shows some of the delivery vehicles in use at that time.

Workers are seen using some interesting looking machinery to make swiss rolls in the 1950s.

A time before the age of automation. Women are seen hand finishing cakes in the chocolate enrober section in the 1950s.

Slab cake mixing in progress. An assistant awaits the mixture which will be taken on to the ovens. This photograph shows the process in the 1950s.

Staff operating the slab cake ovens in the 1950s.

WHITBREAD & CO LTD · BOTTLING STORE

Whitbread's Penarth Road Depot opened as a bottling store in May 1932. It was famous for fulfilling huge orders for the liners *Queen Elizabeth* and *Queen Mary* prior to its closure in 1963. Currently, it is the base for Track 2000 the community recycling organization.

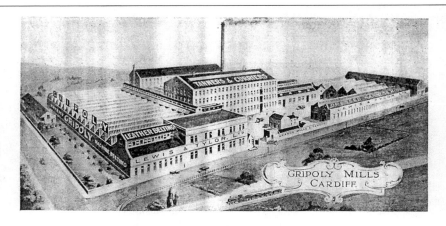

CARDIFF—THE BIRTHPLACE OF "GRIPOLY"

N O record of Cardiff's industries would be complete without reference to what is probably one of the largest and most up-to-date Woven Belting Factories in Great Britain.

Gripoly Mills, Grangetown, Cardiff, is a large and modern works on model lines, and familiar to many as the source of production of the well-known " GRIPOLY " PATENT SOLID WOVEN HAIR BELTS.

" Gripoly " Driving Belts are well-known by reason of their unique guarantees, their world-wide use, and the policy of SERVICE which is always associated with the word " Gripoly."

The unique features surrounding the guaranteed qualities of " Gripoly " Belting and other Gripoly products are as follows :—

The raw materials are guaranteed to be as near perfection as constant testing and inspection to rigid specification can make them.

The buyer of a Gripoly Belt can obtain definite written guarantes, periodically brought up to date, that the Hair Yarns which carry the loads of a Gripoly Belt are made of real camel hair, and that this hair is 100% pure camel.

" GRIPOLY " BELTS are also guaranteed free from defects of material and workmanship, and to give satisfactory service in use.

They are made in a model works under ideal conditions both as regards the workers and the productions made.

The foregoing explains why " GRIPOLY " BELTING is used all over the world, and especially in climates where only the best quality of belting can stand up to the adverse conditions.

It also justifies the established use of " Gripoly " Belting under the severest conditions at home, and explains its standardisation for DROP STAMP work, as well as for general purposes, by many of the leading manufacturers in this country.

Lewis & Tylers Gripoly Mills were situated at Penarth Road and Sloper Road and were renowned for their woven industrial belting and leather products.

Ivor Williams, who owned the Clarence Dairy in Paget Street, is seen here delivering milk on his specially adapted bicycle in 1981.

The picture on this advertisement card for the local haulage company E. Vincent & Sons was taken outside Frank's Sweet Factory in Pendyris Street in the 1920s.

Three
Schooldays

A girls' class at Court Road School smile in 1939, sadly unaware of the forthcoming war .

Grangetown Board School in Bromsgrove Street, built by the Cardiff School Board, served lower Grangetown and is pictured just after opening in 1884.

Large collars were the fashion for the infant's class at Grangetown Board School around 1920.

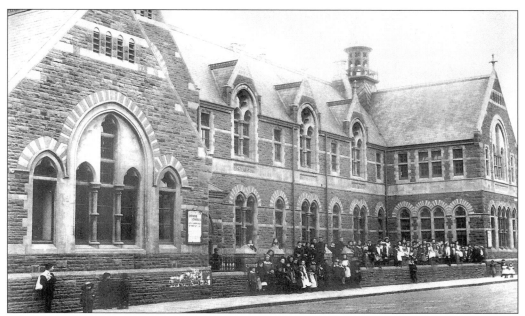

Due to a growing local population, the Grangetown Board School needed to be expanded in 1894 and this view shows the extension to the front elevation of the school.

The Grangetown Board School rugby team proudly pose with their trophies for the 1907/8 season.

There are very few smiles here from the top class of Grangetown Council Infant's School in 1919.

White smocks for the girls class at Grangetown Board School in 1920.

Grange Council School baseball team, Cup and League winners, 1922.

Grange Council baseball team pose with their trophies at Grange Gardens in 1923.

A mixed class at Grange Council School in 1930.

Grange Council baseball team, the undefeated Cup and League winners, 1932/3 and 1933/4.

Grange Council baseball team, League & Cup winners, 1933.

Grange Council School, 1935/6.

Grange Council School baseball team in 1945.

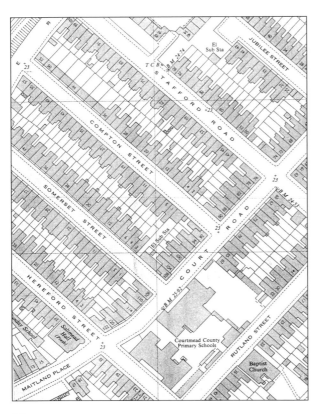

Court Road School was renamed
Courtmead County Primary School
as seen in this 1968 plan.

Children pose at the entrance to Court Road School for the photographer in the early years of this century. It opened on the 14 August 1893 as Court Road School but was renamed Courtmead County Primary School in 1950 when the City Council removed all road and street names from school names. The school was closed in July 1969 and was subsequently demolished in August 1970.

A girls' class at Court Road School photographed by the Home & Colonial Photo Co. of Cardiff, Plymouth and Johannesburg, c. 1902.

A school photograph of a girls' class at Court Road School, *c*. 1904.

Court Road School rugby team in the 1920/1 season.

Standard 1a at Court Road School in 1931.

An infants' class at Court Road School in 1933.

Standard 3 at Court Road School in 1936.

Court Road School in 1944.

A girls' class at Court Road School in the 1950s.

The girls' baseball team at Court Road School in 1956.

The boys' baseball team at Court Road School in 1956.

Ninian Park School boys' class, 1911. The school opened as Virgil Street Board School on 30 November 1900 but the name was changed to Ninian Park Council School in October 1911.

Ninian Park School gymnastic team, 1948.

Ninian Park School football team in 1953/4.

Ninian Park football team in the 1957/8 season.

The last staff of Ninian Park High School in 1968. The headmaster, Mr R.B. Jones, is seated in the centre of the front row.

Grangetown National School in 1929. This Church of England School was built in Clive Street and, after redevelopment in recent years, has changed its name to St Paul's Church In Wales school.

Pupils from Grangetown National School in 1948.

Pupils from Grangetown National School, 1948.

A plan of Grangetown National
School in 1954.

Four

Churches

The Grangetown Corps of the Salvation Army pictured in 1920.

Paget Street Congregational Church was built in 1888 was demolished in the 1970s.

Clare Road Congregational Church opened in June 1886. The Mission Hall, seen on the left, was built in 1889 at a cost of £350. The frontage of this building remains unchanged and is now the premises of H. Tempest Photography.

Grangetown Baptist Church, founded in 1865, continues to serve the community today.

Within the last fifteen years it became necessary to demolish the schoolrooms of Grangetown Baptist Church because of structural problems and the site has since been redeveloped and flats built in place of the church.

Revd John Williams (marked with an x) can be seen with the Grangetown Baptist Church choir on an outing, *c.* 1905.

The men's fellowship of Grangetown Baptist Church on an outing to Tintern in 1905.

Grangetown Baptist Church's Whitsun treat in 1912. The Whitsun treat was an annual picnic for the congregation in the countryside held on Whit Monday.

The bible class of Grangetown Baptist Church at their Whitsun treat, 1917.

The Revd Hopkin Morgan leads the Harvest Festival celebration at Grangetown Baptist Church, c. 1926/7.

The working party of Grangetown Baptist Church prepare to leave for the annual Whitsun treat to Swanbridge in 1955.

Another view of the Grangetown Baptist Church Whitsun treat workers being given a helping hand to leave Clive Street for Swanbridge in 1955.

A Musical Treat

Grangetown S.A. Brass Band.

On MONDAY, Dec. 3rd, 1894,

✕ A MUSICAL FESTIVAL ✕

IN THE

CLIVE HALL, KENT STREET,

On behalf of the funds of the above Band.

The Band will play some special selections, besides a varied programme of Vocal and Instrumental Music, Childrens' Songs, Recitations, &c.

To commence at 8 sharp.

Tickets, - - Threepence each.

ADAMS, BELFAST.

This advertising poster of 1894 shows that the Grangetown Salvation Army Band raised funds for the band by holding concerts in their hall in Kent Street.

The Salvation Army Band pose outside Clive Hall in Kent Street. A poster on the wall reads 'Self Denial Week, 1901'.

Grangetown Salvation Army Scout Group in 1952.

Avondale Crescent in 1954 … and the Grangetown Salvation Army Band play on!

Dr Rhoden, a well-respected local GP was presented with the key to open the new Salvation Army Hall (formerly Salem Baptist Chapel) in Corporation Road in 1956.

A Sunday School class from Ebenezer Gospel Hall, Corporation Road, 1936/7. Ron Watkiss, fifth from the left, back row, would later go on to become Lord Mayor of Cardiff and Harry Mansfield, third from the left, back row, became City Treasurer.

Ebenezer Gospel Hall infant's class, 1950.

The Ebenezer Gospel Hall Mission, held on The Marl in the early 1950s, attracted many local youngsters.

Penarth Road Methodist Church, situated on the corner of Penarth Road and Clare Road, is seen in 1912 when traffic was scarce.

Over sixty years later the church closed due to a dwindling congregation and was waiting to be demolished before it was gutted by fire in the late 1970s.

A lone fireman is seen after the fire had been finally controlled, but the building had been gutted. The site was later redeveloped and a supermarket was built there.

The sisterhood of Saltmead Hall, situated on the corner of Hereford Street and Maitland Place, are about to depart on a charabanc outing in the 1920s.

Cornwall Road (Street) Baptist Church, which was founded in 1894, still serves the local community today and is currently planning complete modernization to face the new millennium.

Five

Celebrations

What better way is there for neighbours to celebrate good times than to stage a street party, such as this seen most recently, at Ferry Road in 1953, to celebrate the Coronation of Queen Elizabeth II.

The residents of Hewell Street had quite a party in 1937 to commemorate the Coronation of King George VI and Queen Elizabeth.

The ladies of Hewell Street are seen enjoying themselves at the 1937 Coronation street party.

Party hats and decorations cheer the residents of Warwick Street at their Coronation celebrations in 1937.

The child in the pram seems more interested looking at the table than the photographer at the VE Day (victory in Europe day) celebrations on Taff Embankment, 1945.

The party is about to begin for the residents of Monmouth Street as they celebrate VE Day in May 1945.

The residents of Ludlow Street celebrating VJ (victory over Japan) Day in 1945.

Sunshine and smiles at the VJ Day party in Oakley Street 15 August 1945.

8th June, 1946

TO-DAY, AS WE CELEBRATE VICTORY, I send this personal message to you and all other boys and girls at school. For you have shared in the hardships and dangers of a total war and you have shared no less in the triumph of the Allied Nations.

I know you will always feel proud to belong to a country which was capable of such supreme effort; proud, too, of parents and elder brothers and sisters who by their courage, endurance and enterprise brought victory. May these qualities be yours as you grow up and join in the common effort to establish among the nations of the world unity and peace.

George R.I

A message from the King to all schoolchildren in 1946 celebrating the end of the Second World War.

Mrs Violet Isitt of Ferndale Street joins the local one-man-band for a dance.

Preparations are made to celebrate the Coronation of Queen Elizabeth II in Llanmaes Street in 1953.

The 1953 Coronation street party in Llanmaes Street.

Another view of Llanmaes Street Coronation party in 1953.

The children of Hereford Street enjoying the Coronation party in 1953.

Six
Transport

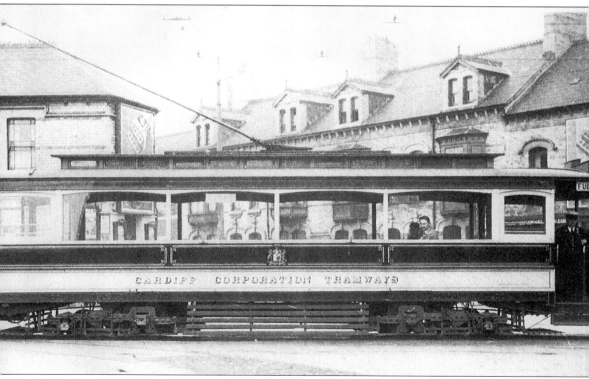

A Cardiff Corporation Tramways single deck tram seen near the Clare Road Tram Depot in 1939.

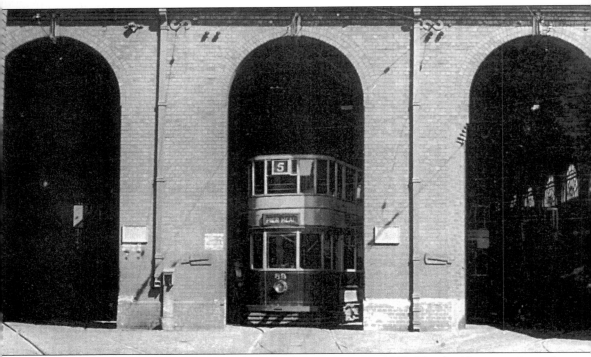

A No. 5 tram about to leave the Clare Road Tram Depot in 1939. This building remains today and is used by the Maintenance Department of Cardiff County Council.

The Cardiff Corporation Electric Tramways fitting and cleaning staff at Clare Road Tram Depot, c. 1900.

An open-top tram bound for Clifton Street leaves the Clare Road Depot in the late 1930s.

A Cardiff Corporation trolleybus on the Llandaff Fields to Pier Head route seen outside the Clare Road Depot in 1949.

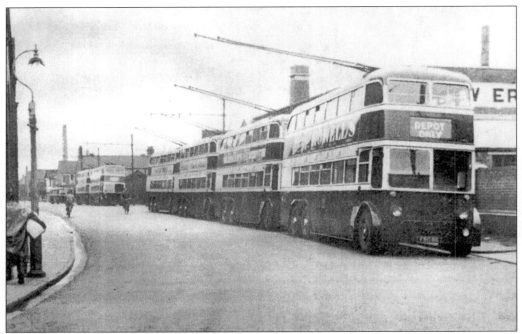

Some of the Cardiff Corporation trolleybus fleet parked in Pendyris Street alongside the Clare Road Depot in the 1950s.

A Taff Vale Railway 'autotrain' calls at Grangetown station, in 1907, before proceeding to Penarth. The autotrain consisted of a steam train between two carriages.

Great Western Railway staff at Grangetown station in the 1920s.

The Grangetown signal box as seen in the 1940s. Positioned near Grangetown railway station, it controlled the signals and points for the lines to the Ferry Road area and the Barry/Penarth line.

A Cardiff to Penarth British Rail steam train calling at Grangetown station on the 2 May 1958.

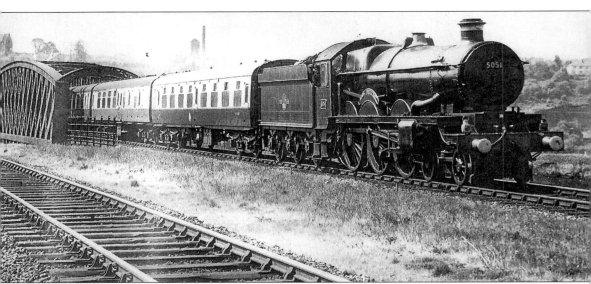

An express train diverted via the Vale of Glamorgan line approaches Grangetown on Sunday 4 May 1958. To enable track maintenance work to take place on the Cardiff to Swansea main line it was common for express trains to be diverted via the Vale of Glamorgan through Barry to rejoin the main line at Cardiff.

Seven

Sport and Recreation

Lewis & Tyler's Gripoly Mills ladies' baseball team are all smiles after a winning season in 1924.

Grange Gardens, a well loved public park, is pictured before the First World War.

Local residents enjoy watching a game of bowls at Grange Gardens, *c.* 1912.

A young lad kneels to tie his shoelace in this 1910 view of Grange Gardens, while a group of children line up in front of the bandstand. An undeveloped Corporation Road can be seen at the boundary of the park to the left.

A winter scene in Grange Gardens looking towards the Louis Samuel memorial fountain erected in 1909.

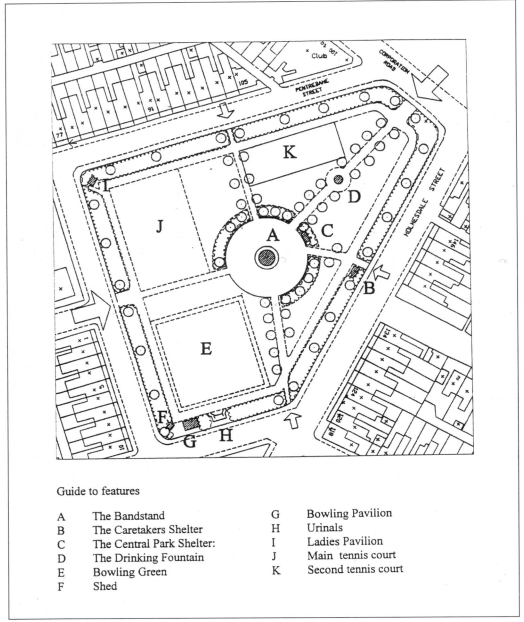

Guide to features

A	The Bandstand	G	Bowling Pavilion
B	The Caretakers Shelter	H	Urinals
C	The Central Park Shelter:	I	Ladies Pavilion
D	The Drinking Fountain	J	Main tennis court
E	Bowling Green	K	Second tennis court
F	Shed		

A plan of Grange Gardens, c. 1918.

Grangetown Conservative Club baseball team pictured in front of the bandstand in Grange Gardens at a later date than indicated on the photograph (1892) because the bandstand was not erected until 1895. Left to right, back row: B. Henderson, T. Duffy, C. Herbert, F. Newswag, C. Noyse, E. Barry. Middle row: B. Smith, J. Evans, D. Morgan, I. Cavill, S. Andrews, P. Ryan. Front row: G. Cullen, A. Chappell, J. Spavin (captain), F. Smith, J. Lewis, W. Dobson. At the front: T. Mabbs, E. Moorcraft.

The bandstand in Grange Gardens was removed over forty years ago. However there are plans to restore this feature to the park, in 1999, with funds from the national lottery.

Grangetown Bowls Club in the 1950s.

The committee of the Grange Temperance Institute which was situated at The Square, Holmesdale Street, *c.* 1924/5. The Temperance Institute later became Grange Albion.

Grange Albion Baseball Club, winners of the Welsh League and Dewar Shield 1921/2, Grange Cup 1921/2, Welsh Cup 1922, Express Bowl 1922.

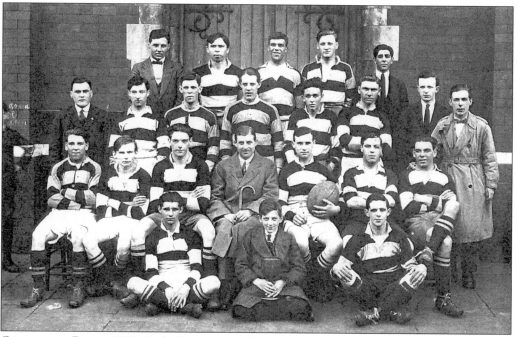

Grangetown Baptist RFC 2nd XV, 1919/20. The president, Lt Harry Turner, is seated centre alongside the captain, G.H. Cornish.

Grangetown Baptist RFC, 1920/1. The captain A. Hobbs can be seen wearing the cap and the president, Lt Harry Turner, is seated in the centre.

Ninian Villa AFC, 1929/30.

Grange Stars AFC, 1931/2.

Sussex Bantams soccer team from Sussex Street, 1921/2.

Grange Vics FC, 1937/8.

Grange Albion baseball team in the 1920s.

St Patrick's FC, 1962/3.

The Cardiff Gas Boxing Club in 1933. Pictured, left to right, are: Wilfred Bryant, Don O'Leary and Cyril Gallie. They were the winners of the Welsh Schools' and British Youth Championship Shields.

Cyril Gallie was a local boxer who became Welsh Schoolboy Champion in 1934, and went on to win other titles including British Featherweight Champion in 1938 and 1939.

Cardiff Gas Boxing Club pictured at the Cardiff Coke & Gas Company sportsground, Ferry Road, in 1935.

Cardiff Gasworks Boxing Club in the late 1950s. David 'Darkie' Hughes, British Lightweight Champion in 1960, can be seen third from left on the back row.

Cardiff Gas Boxing Club outside their St Barnabas Hall training headquarters in 1952.

Fred Hayes of Grange Albion
baseball team in 1956.

Grange Albion baseball team at Sevenoaks Park in 1958.

Eight
People and Events

Two newspaper delivery men pose outside Syl Evans' newsagent shop at Clare Road, *c.* 1920.
Note that the *News of the World* newspaper cost only one penny!

J.R. Freeman's Cigar Factory girls show solidarity by joining the Seaman's strike in 1911. The factory was situated in North Clive Street.

Freeman's Cigar Factory outing to Symonds Yat in July 1926.

Another Freeman's Cigar Factory charabanc outing, this time to Abergavenny in 1926.

Coach driver Thomas George Jones of Grangetown, who was employed by the Queen's Hotel in St Mary Street, is pictured outside the Sophia Gardens Lodge at the turn of the century.

The funeral of the young wife of the Salvation Army captain, in 1927, was a sad occasion and many local residents paid their respects to the cortège as it passed through Holmesdale Street.

The funeral procession continues along Holmesdale Street.

The Guitar, Mandolin and Banjo Club was based at the YMCA Clydach Street in 1934. This talented band of thirty local musicians were much sought after the concerts in the Cardiff area.

The YMCA building in Clydach Street continues to serve the local community and is currently the base of Grangetown Community Concern who operate a day centre for local senior citizens.

PC Frank Brookes of Penarth Road spent most of his working life at Clive Street police station before passing away in 1938.

The Whitsun outing of the Grangetown Conservative Club in the 1930s.

Bombardier Owen Lewis Nurton was awarded the Distinguished Service Medal for bravery without regard for his own life when he rescued fellow soldiers while under enemy fire during the First World War. He was presented with a gold watch and chain by local dignitaries outside Penarth Road Presbyterian Forward Movement Hall, a ceremony witnessed by a large gathering of the local community.

Bombardier Nurton received a hero's welcome when he returned to his home in Stockland Street.

Flt Eng. James Norris of Mardy Street served in the RAF during the Second World War and was awarded the Conspicuous Gallantry Medal. Although he had had no formal flying experience, he managed to pilot a Lancaster bomber back to Britain single-handedly after the crew were injured after a bombing raid on Germany.

An engraved watch was presented to Flt Eng. James Norris at Cambridge Street Clinic in 1944. The presentation was made by Councillor Gabriel Shute and watched by Councillor Helena Evans and Councillor E. Cazenave.

Will Dungey, who served aboard HMS *Iron Duke* during the First World War, is pictured with his younger brother in 1917.

Local councillors Gabriel Shute (second left, front row), Helena Evans (fourth from the left, front row) and E. Cazenave (fifth from the left, front row) with fellow organizers leave Grangetown Baptist Church after a 'Holidays at Home' meeting in 1946. Arrangements were made for local entertainment during the first summer after the Second World War.

Frank Davison and his band pictured at the Regent Ballroom in Mardy Street in the 1950s.

Grangetown-born Dan Donovan was a
popular singer on the radio and in concert.
His career stretched through a thirty-year
period from 1920.

The Regency Dance Band, seen at St Patrick's Hall, comprised of, left to right, Ted Brown,
George Evans, Dennis Ranson, George Ranson, Doris Ranson, Ernie Miller, Doris Bennett.

The Jubilee Club darts team in the 1950s.

Members of the Jubilee Club, Penarth Road are pictured in North Clive Street prior to a coach outing in the 1950s.

The ladies of Hewell Street about to depart on an outing in the 1950s.

The Bird In Hand pub darts team, *c.* 1955.

The children of Hereford Street show off their new uniforms for the return to school in 1952.

A group of lads are seen here playing in Gillard's field, which later became Sevenoaks Park. Lewis & Tylers Gripoly Mills can be seen in the backround of this 1915 view.

Grangetown Baptist Girl Guides and Guide Leader, Edith Shute (centre right), are seen at Cardiff General Station before embarking on a camping holiday to Switzerland in 1958.

Mr Gabriel Shute of Penhevad Street represented Grangetown as an Independent councillor for seventeen years.

The council chamber of City Hall where Grangetown-born Harry Mansfield welcomed the Queen and the Duke of Edinburgh during their Silver Jubilee visit to Cardiff in 1977.

The women's section of the local Labour Party on an outing to Gloucester arranged by local Labour Party agent Mrs Hatto in 1938.

Lord Mayor Alderman George Ferrier is seen at a City Hall event in 1954. Alderman Ferrier ran a wholesale grocery business from North Clive Street.

Drivers and buses in Pentrebane Street for the Grangetown Conservative Club outing, *c.* 1949.

Sevenoaks Park Youth Club was run by Mrs Chard in 1956.

In 1979, due to the high level of water in the River Taff, the Clare Road area was subject to flooding as these photographs show. Anti-flood prevention work undertaken since by the Water Authority should ensure that this does not happen again.

Acknowledgements

I would like to thank the many people who offered information and photographs for use in this publication. Especially: Eileen Breslin, Denise and Louise Carson, Betty Casella, Jean Clatworthy, Billy Dadd, Christine Davies (Grangetown Community Concern), Peter Farr, Peggy Harris, Dolly King, Thomas Maclean, Jim Norris, Joan Nurton, Glyn Paul, Gareth Phillips (Cardiff Parks Dept), Peter Ranson, Ray Shaw, Edith Shute, Rita Spinola, Ann Stockford, Edith Thomas, Gwyn Thomas, Grangetown Local History Society members, Mark Bailey and the staff at Grangetown Library, Grangetown Conservative Club, Grangetown Salvation Army, Grangetown Baptist Church. To all who I have failed to mention please accept my apologies.

Special thanks are due to Alun Richards and Steve Williams for their help and expertise with the word processing. Finally a word of thanks to Veronica Simpson for her help and support at a time when this book became difficult to complete.

If anyone has photographs they think may be of interest I would ask that you come along to the Grangetown Local History Society meetings held monthly at Grangetown Library where you will receive a warm welcome.